Elf~help
for Overcoming
Depression

D1432486

Elf~help
for Overcoming
Depression

written by
Linus Mundy

illustrated by
R.W. Alley

ONE
CARING
PLACE

Abbey Press

Text © 1998 by Linus Mundy
Illustrations © 1998 by St. Meinrad Archabbey
Published by One Caring Place
Abbey Press
St. Meinrad, Indiana 47577

All rights reserved.
No part of this book may be used or reproduced in any manner
without written permission of the publisher, except in the case of
brief quotations embodied in critical articles and reviews.

Library of Congress Catalog Number
98-71232

ISBN 0-87029-315-X

Printed in the United States of America

Foreword

Living with an occasional "bad day" is one thing, but living from day to day in a blue funk can be devastating. The popular saying goes: "Only *you* can make you happy," yet that's only partly true. When we're down and out, our fellow human beings are there to help us, more than we ever know. Beyond that, our faith tells us squarely that we can ask for—and expect—*divine* help, too.

That doesn't mean we can simply "cheer up" or "snap out of it." Addressing the problem—figuring out exactly what we can do about our feelings of hopelessness—begins with information and understanding. What's normal? What isn't? How did all of this start? What are the underlying causes? What's the "treatment" that works? What *doesn't* work?

Elf-help for Overcoming Depression distills much borrowed and hard-won wisdom on all of these tough questions. The thirty-eight short insights that follow will reassure you that *there is hope*...and that help can come from a lot of great sources.

1.

Feeling down is a natural reaction to life's hurts, stresses, changes, and disappointments. The road to taking action and feeling well again begins with self-awareness: understanding depression and realizing just where you are.

2.

Most of us were taught, as children, how to tie our shoes and ride a bike and blow our nose or read a book. But we weren't taught the intricacies of managing our emotions. It's not too late to learn how to manage your emotions competently.

3.

Information is your best weapon against depression. Learn all you can about its causes, types, treatments.

4.

We come to know ourselves
well only after we've brushed
up against a lot of adversity.
Rather than being threatened
by depression, see it as a
springboard to personal
growth and self-understanding.

5.

Depression is an illness of the body, mind, and spirit. To treat it, you must pay attention to all of you. Where are you hurting? Ask yourself how you can bring healing to that part of your life.

6.

Because depression frequently has physical causes and effects, to really "cheer up" or "snap out of it" often requires medical assistance. Turn to the experts who can help you treat it and defeat it.

7.

Experts tell us that we act and react according to preset tapes in our head—using thinking and behaving patterns acquired in childhood. But since these patterns are learned, they can be un-learned. Start giving yourself new, positive, and affirming messages.

8.

Most of life is neither perfect nor terrible, totally black nor totally white. Expect constant change in your life, and occasional chaos. Expect that life, while not fair, can still be good.

9.

While you may think it's raining on you, it's quite possibly just raining. Look at the bigger picture, and be open to adjusting your attitude if need be.

10.

Don't let your life be too full of <u>musts</u>, <u>shoulds</u>, and <u>have-to's</u>. You do have choices. Let your values and priorities shape your daily life.

11.

If you're always pushing toward greater success, achievement, control, perfection, and efficiency, you're overrating greatness—as well as your own human capacities. You're great because of who you are, not because of what you can do.

12.

Feeling helpless or trapped is one of the main reasons people get depressed. Be sure to spend as much time thinking about positive solutions as you do thinking about how helpless you feel.

13.

Sometimes we get into the habit of "awful-izing." It's okay to ask yourself: "What's the worst thing that could happen?" But be sure to balance this with: "What's the best thing that could happen?"

14.

Feelings of hopelessness can come from feeling overwhelmed, as if you're buried under an avalanche. You can't push all the rubble away at once. You need to remove the rocks one at a time. (And maybe with the help of someone else.)

15.

When a too-heavy burden
flattens your wheels, you may
think you have no options.
But in reality there are many:
remove some weight, put more
air in your tires, get help, delay
your delivery, get some rest
and see things from a new
perspective.

16.

Put "Have fun" on your "To do" list. Sure, fun is mostly spontaneous, but some of it has to be planned.

17.

Picture yourself as a happy person, filled with grace and love. Regardless of who you are, or what you have or haven't done, you can work at being a calm and gentle spirit living in inner peace.

18.

It's okay to be you. As a matter of fact, being you is the only person you will be good at being. Cherish the "you" that God created. Believe in yourself; recognize your own worth. Joy and peace grow out of feeling competent and confident.

19.

Listen to the voice deepest within you. That's your heart speaking. Your heart knows it's love that matters most and love that brings peace and hope.

20.

Children know a simple secret
about joy: It's the little things
that are the big things. Observe
children at work and play—
and, like them, look for everyday
small ways to have fun.

21.

If you feel like you need a miracle in your life, you probably do. Ask for one. But remember that miracles can be small. Sometimes you just need to notice the ones God has put right in front of you.

22.

Nature carries a basketful of pick-me-ups. Smell, taste, touch its contents regularly.

23.

Don't underestimate the power of creativity to lift you out of the fog. Sing a song, bake a cobbler, paint a picture, compose a poem, build a birdhouse.

24.

Exercise—movement in general—can give you a new perspective on things. At the very least, you will have a physical outlet for bottled-up anxieties...and you will generally sleep and rest better.

25.

When something looks good,
sounds good, feels good, tastes
good, smells good...say so. It's a
happy habit to have. Counting
your blessings is good therapy.

26.

Look toward the future—
especially during the holidays,
when people are often busy
trying to recapture that perfect
past of the good old days. Better
yet, take satisfaction in who
you are, where you are, what
you are doing right now!

27.

Get the spotlight off yourself—
by shining it onto someone or
something else: a hobby or craft,
a garden or pet, a neighbor or
relative, a needy person or
project.

28.

Sometimes you can't climb up from depression all by yourself. There are people who are glad to throw you a rope, give you a needed boost, pick you up and carry you to a better place. Let them.

29.

Depression is highly treatable. Physicians and therapists can help you to get the insights, coping skills, or medication you need to overcome it. If your depression is severe or persistent, turn to an expert and together work out a plan to get well again.

30.

Don't let pride keep you from reaching out to your neighbor, your church, your spouse, your teacher, your friend, your doctor, your God. A big part of depression is feeling so alone. Accept the help and encouragement others can give you.

31.

If at times you can't seem to ask for help, look for expressions of kindness anyway: a pat on the back, a knowing smile or grin or glance during a tough time. Notice these gentle gestures. They are intended for you and can shore you up.

32.

You may feel that no one could possibly understand what you are going through right now. You're probably right. But others can still help. Ask for what you need. You'll be surprised how often you get it.

33.

Friendship doubles our joy and divides our grief. Find someone—or Someone—to share your deepest feelings and worries with.

34.

Listen to the wisdom of the wounded. Their pain may no longer be as intense as yours, but the perspective they bring can lessen your feelings of hopelessness and despair.

35.

Don't get discouraged if you don't feel better immediately. You may be improving even though you don't yet feel it. The main thing is to continue to take steps toward healing and to reject negative thinking.

36.

Let God into your life. With God along, you can bear the unbearable. And even life's best things get better.

37.

Don't buy into the self-defeating myth that if only your faith were stronger you would be exempt from depression. God and religion don't work that way. Remind yourself that God loves you but you are human and you live in an imperfect world.

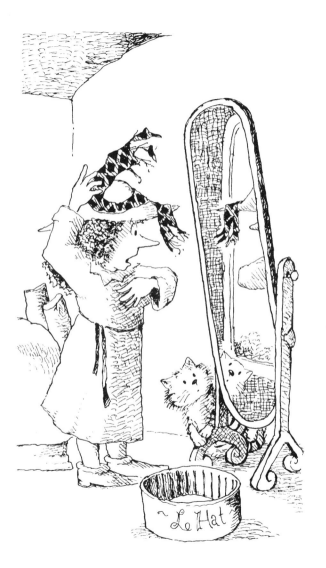

38.

God has promised us peace and fullness of life. We can help God help us to climb up from depression by accepting as our motto: "Treat <u>it</u> and defeat <u>it</u>!"

Linus Mundy has written a number of Elf-help Books including *Slow-down Therapy* and *Grief Therapy for Men.* He is director of the publications program at Abbey Press known as One Caring Place. Married and the father of three children, he is also author of the book, *Prayer-Walking.*

Illustrator for the Abbey Press Elf-help Books, **R.W. Alley** also illustrates and writes children's books. He lives in Barrington, Rhode Island, with his wife, daughter, and son.

The Story of the Abbey Press Elves

The engaging figures that populate the Abbey Press "elf-help" line of publications and products first appeared in 1987 on the pages of a small self-help book called *Be-good-to-yourself Therapy*. Shaped by the publishing staff's vision and defined in R.W. Alley's inventive illustrations, they lived out author Cherry Hartman's gentle, self-nurturing advice with charm, poignancy, and humor.

Reader response was so enthusiastic that more Elf-help Books were soon under way, a still-growing series that has inspired a line of related gift products.

The especially endearing character featured in the early books—sporting a cap with a mood-changing candle in its peak—has since been joined by a spirited female elf with flowers in her hair.

These two exuberant, sensitive, resourceful, kindhearted, lovable sprites, along with their lively elfin community, reveal what's truly important as they offer messages of joy and wonder, playfulness and co-creation, wholeness and serenity, the miracle of life and the mystery of God's love.

With wisdom and whimsy, these little creatures with long noses demonstrate the elf-help way to a rich and fulfilling life.

Elf-help Books

...adding "a little character" and a lot of help to self-help reading!

Healing Thoughts for Troubled Hearts	#20058
Take Charge of Your Eating	#20064
Elf-help for Coping With Pain	#20074
Elf-help for Dealing with Difficult People	#20076
Loneliness Therapy	#20078
Nature Therapy	#20080
Elf-help for Healing from Divorce	#20082
Music Therapy	#20083
Elf-help for a Happy Retirement	#20085
'Tis a Blessing to Be Irish	#20088
Getting Older, Growing Wiser	#20089
Worry Therapy	#20093
Elf-help for Raising a Teen	#20102
Elf-help for Being a Good Parent	#20103
Gratitude Therapy	#20105
Trust-in-God Therapy	#20119

Elf-help for Overcoming Depression	#20134
New Baby Therapy	#20140
Teacher Therapy	#20145
Stress Therapy	#20153
Making-sense-out-of-suffering Therapy	#20156
Get Well Therapy	#20157
Anger Therapy	#20127
Caregiver Therapy	#20164
Self-esteem Therapy	#20165
Peace Therapy	#20176
Friendship Therapy	#20174
Christmas Therapy (color edition) $5.95	#20175
Grief Therapy	#20178
Happy Birthday Therapy	#20181
Forgiveness Therapy	#20184
Keep-life-simple Therapy	#20185
Celebrate-your-womanhood Therapy	#20189
Acceptance Therapy (color edition) $5.95	#20182
Acceptance Therapy	#20190

Book price is $4.95 unless otherwise noted.
Available at your favorite giftshop or bookstore—
or directly from One Caring Place, Abbey Press
Publications, St. Meinrad, IN 47577.
Or call 1-800-325-2511.
www.carenotes.com